# History of Preston

## *An Introduction*

ALISTAIR C. HODGE

Carnegie Publishing, 1997

History of Preston: An Introduction
Alistair C. Hodge

Published by Carnegie Publishing Ltd
18 Maynard Street, Preston PR2 2AL

First edition published in 1984

Copyright © Alistair Hodge, 1984, 1997

Typeset in Monotype Fournier
Printed and bound in the UK by Cambridge University Press

*British Library Cataloguing in Publication Data*
A CIP record for this book is available from the British Library

ISBN 1-85936-049-1

# Contents

# *Preface*

 s a Scot by birth, I think perhaps I should apologise. First for presuming to write a history of a Lancashire town and, second, for the appalling behaviour of certain of my ancestors. They did, after all, sack and loot Preston at least twice, and they fought major battles here on at least another two occasions. As far as I know, none of my direct forebears was responsible.

This history, as its title implies, is no more than a short introduction to Preston's past and makes little enough claim to scholarship. It owes a great deal to the work of others, far too numerous to mention individually here. Many things have had to be omitted, and much is left untold. In particular, greater space would have allowed a fuller treatment of recent events than has been possible here.

Among many others I would like to thank the staffs of the Lancashire Record Office and the Harris Reference Library for their very great help. Thanks also are due to Professors Austin Woolrych and John Walton of Lancaster University for their support and encouragement. The mistakes in this work, however, are very much my own.

It seems such a long time since the first edition of this little work was delivered – by bicycle – to Sweetens bookshop on Fishergate in the summer of 1984. Then it was the first title of a new imprint, Carnegie Press. Now it has the honour of following in the wake of a much grander and more eloquent history of the town by Dr David Hunt, published to coincide with Preston Guild in 1992, and also released by Carnegie, in conjunction with the borough council. Historiography has moved forward, too, although I cannot claim to have made use of more than a tiny proportion of the new work that has been done by several eminent local historians such as Alan Crosby, David Hunt, Nigel Morgan and Geoff Timmins.

Still, I hope that as a brief and hopefully readable introduction to the subject there is yet a place on local bookshelves for this little book.

Alistair Hodge, March 1994

# *Introduction*

RESTON'S HISTORY begins about 1,200 years ago. This fact alone may surprise many people who have noticed the relative lack of old buildings in the town today. It can hardly be said of Preston that its townscape reflects its antiquity. Entering the town by any of the main roads – Garstang Road, Fishergate Hill or New Hall Lane – there are few enough clues to historical events dating back beyond more than 150 years or so.

Yet Preston is one of the oldest boroughs in the county and the church around which the original settlement grew up – St John's at the top of Church Street – may have been one of the earliest in the North West of England, with associations supposedly going back to St Wilfrid early in the eighth century.

The site of the settlement was on a major crossroads and at a major river crossing (being in practice at the lowest point on the Ribble where it is safe and practicable to cross, despite the existence of an ancient ford at Hesketh Bank). From an early date, too, the town's market was one of the most important in the area, and Preston was the county's main legal and administrative centre.

For almost 1,000 years Preston remained, by modern standards, a small rural market town, much admired by visitors for its situation, the wealth of its inhabitants and the high quality of its buildings. Then, in the space of less than a hundred years, the whole nature and character of the town were transformed by the arrival of industry. As in so many other Lancashire towns, cotton mills, rows of terraced housing, the canal, railways, urban sprawl and population boom all contributed to change the physical and social environment of the town literally beyond recognition. From being a fashionable retreat for the county's socialites and gentry, it quickly gained a richly deserved reputation for industrial pollution, dirt and noise – hardly the sort of place for the county set.

It is difficult to overestimate the huge impact which the Industrial Revolution had on Preston. You need only take a stroll along any of the ancient streets – Friargate (from around the Roper Hall); Churchgate, now Church Street (from around Grimshaw Street); and Fishergate (from around Mount Street) and look around you. Only a handful of buildings can be said with

confidence to pre-date the first heroic age of the Industrial Revolution. The great majority, including the parish church, are of much more recent date.

Yet, if you but scratch the surface and look behind the nineteenth- and twentieth-century façades, there is a surprising amount to find: the remains of older buildings, and settlement patterns belonging to an earlier age.

On the main streets of the town the cardinal rule is to look upwards. National retail chains believe that corporate identity is very important, a belief that has made the ground-floor aspects of Fishergate and Friargate almost indistinguishable from those of every other English town. But the upper storeys tell a different tale. Next time you are in the town centre, take a look at buildings such as the TSB opposite the parish church, the Bull & Royal, the former Conservative Club on Guildhall Street, some of the shops on Fishergate and Yates' the jewellers on the Market Square.

# CHAPTER ONE

# *Earliest Preston*

E DO NOT KNOW when the first settlement was built on the site of modern Preston. There is no direct evidence until after Roman times, although it is likely that some archaeological evidence was destroyed during the last century when the town was being extensively rebuilt – nineteenth-century town-centre shops have much deeper cellars and foundations than the buildings they replaced – and some sites in the middle of the town still have not been explored properly.

At present, therefore, our knowledge is limited. There have been several finds which show some human influence in this part of Lancashire perhaps as long ago as 8,000 B.C., and the discovery of some axe- and spear-heads in Preston suggests that there may have been some kind of human habitation here perhaps as early as 5,000 years ago. In particular, Higher Brockholes, Cuerdale and the Flats at Walton-le-Dale look as if they could have been sites of very early human habitation.

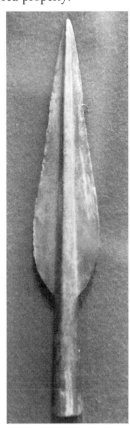

In Roman times, there was certainly a Roman camp of some sort at Walton-le-Dale. Although the military fort at Ribchester (BREMETENNACUM) was always more important, the camp at Walton did lie on a major road northwards, and it overlooked a major river crossing (see Map 1). Recent digs suggest that there may have been a small fort here until the early years of the Flavian period, but a later phase of activity seems to indicate some kind of industrial site or depot for the storage of military or other equipment or supplies for distribution throughout the rest of the region. A permanent settlement here seems unlikely, however, as evidence from the later period of Roman rule is very scanty.

Another ancient, probably Anglian, settlement is said to have been located on Castle Hill in Penwortham. Unlike the Roman camp, this would probably have been built for defensive purposes, on top of an easily fortified natural hill. It, too, lay close to a ford over the river Ribble where, it was said in 1684, the river 'divided into three streams' – because of

Spear head from the Middle Bronze Age. Several similar spears have been found in the area.

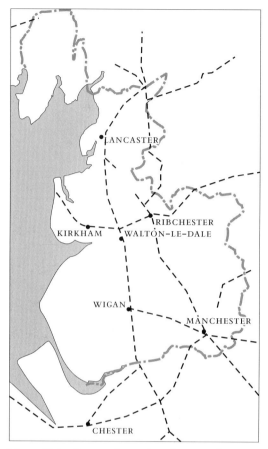

Map 1. Major Roman sites and roads in North-West England. The old county boundary is shown.

Penwortham Holme – and where the ford was 'a very secure passage if the water be not too deep by fresh or flood'.

Preston itself, of course, was founded across the river, near to the northern bank. Very little is known about this early period, but it is probable that the church acted as the nucleus of the later town. One theory says that Preston church was founded by monks from the famous monastery at Ripon in Yorkshire after St Wilfrid acquired the lands 'juxta Rippel' (by the Ribble) for that monastery in about A.D. 670. This would explain why the parish church was originally dedicated to St Wilfrid (until after the Reformation when it became St John's), and probably also how Preston got its name: it is derived from the words 'tun [i.e. town] of the priests'. Besides, St Wilfrid was renowned for his church building, and we know that there were indeed close links with Yorkshire through the kingdom of Northumbria at this time. If this theory is correct, then the Stoneygate site where the modern parish church is situated was one of the earliest Christian sites in the North West.

Why here? We cannot be sure. At this time, the area of central Lancashire north of the Ribble was a part of the Yorkshire-based kingdom of Northumbria, having been taken over under king Ethelfrith (A.D. 593–616), and the Ribble formed a border, albeit

A Bronze coin of Hadrian, found in the river bed during excavations for the Albert Edward Dock in 1886.

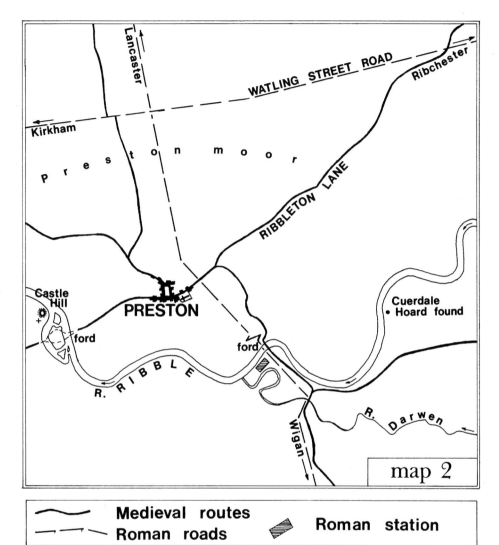

Lancaster

WATLING STREET ROAD

Ribchester

Kirkham

P r e s t o n m o o r

RIBBLETON LANE

Castle Hill

PRESTON

ford

ford

Cuerdale
• Hoard found

R. RIBBLE

R. Darwen

Wigan

map 2

| | |
|---|---|
| 〰 **Medieval routes** | ◈ **Roman station** |
| ⟋⟍ **Roman roads** | |

undefined, with Mercia to the south. Preston may have appeared to be a good site near that border – it lies astride two major roads, one from north to south, the other from west to east, and stands on an attractive bluff which commands an impressive view over the river. Also, the land around the centre of Preston is sandy and therefore much less marshy than many other nearby sites.

It seems likely that most of the early settlers would have been Angles, but these centuries were certainly unsettled and the wide variety of place-name origins in the Preston area and Lancashire as a whole indicates the large number of external influences and migrations which took place. Old British

Coins from the Cuerdale Hoard. (*Private collection*)

names are mixed up with Celtic, Anglian and Scandinavian. Norwegian influence was especially prominent, as in names like Hesketh, Savick, Lund and Salwick. The Norse first came to Lancashire from their bases in Orkney and Shetland early in the ninth century. At first they raided, but later on they settled, and in time, they came to accept the rule of English kings, and were converted to Christianity.

One of the most important Viking remains ever to be found in this country was discovered at Cuerdale, just across the river from Preston. A coin hoard containing no fewer than 7,000 silver coins and other valuables had been buried near the river about the year 903, and during a flood in 1840 the river bank was washed away exposing the hoard to some workmen. The hoard is one of the largest of its kind ever found. It had been suggested that it was the pay chest of some Viking or English king who buried his money rather than allow it to fall into the hands of the enemy. Certainly, there must have been a pressing reason to bury such an immense sum!

We know very little about Preston and the surrounding area during this period. Some historians have taken this lack of evidence to mean that there was no settlement here until much later. But when Preston is first mentioned, in the eleventh century, it was already the most important town in Amounderness (that area of central Lancashire between the rivers Ribble and Cocker, including the Fylde and Bowland), and it is therefore probable that the town had already been established for some time by then.

# CHAPTER TWO

# Medieval Preston

N THE LONG TERM, the Norman invasion and conquest of 1066 brought a greater degree of peace and stability to most of England. In the north, however, these benefits were less obvious, and Lancashire remained troubled and unsettled. In about 1061, Malcolm III (who had defeated and killed Macbeth for the Scottish throne) invaded the North West on a 'bloodthirsty shopping trip', stealing cattle and other moveables, and laying waste to much of north Lancashire as far south as Preston.

Amounderness was sparsely populated at this time, and Preston was certainly small, with no more than a few hundred inhabitants at the most. The town – little more than a large village by modern standards – would have been built almost entirely of wood (not a red brick in sight!), and it may have had some primitive fortifications, though no evidence of these has been found. Physically the town was cut off. About half a mile to the south of Preston ran the Ribble. There was marsh to the west and near the river. The large areas of moor to the north and east were 'replenished with high fir trees', as a visitor noted in 1535; Fulwood was almost entirely covered in forest. This, together with the poor state of the roads, and with the Pennines and the sea further afield, tended to make Preston and Lancashire as a whole relatively isolated and introverted – it was described as a 'dark corner of the land' even as late as the seventeenth century.

Stonework from the small Franciscan friary which was founded around 1221 on Mount Pleasant, just west of Friargate.

Preston's position was favourable, though. An ancient road ran through Warrington, Wigan and Preston to Cockersand, Lancaster and further north. This became busier as both population and trade increased during the High Middle Ages of the twelfth and thirteenth centuries. The port on the river at Preston also helped increase the trade of the town, for although it was never very important, it did cater for increasing numbers of small vessels. The town also stood right at the heart of

It's amazing what you can see if you look from a different angle. This photograph was taken in 1997 from the top level of St George's Centre car park, looking north towards Friargate. The narrow buildings and strips of land running back from the main street are the medieval burgage plots – short street frontages with long, narrow plots of land behind, each owned or part-owned by a burgess who was legally entitled to trade in the town. It is a landholding pattern that can still be seen on the south side of Church Street and Fishergate, where narrow streets like Butlers Court and Main Sprit Weind still follow their medieval lines.

Lancashire's arable land, and was as a consequence the county's most important agricultural market.

Because of this, Preston was probably the first town in Lancashire to receive a formal royal grant of the right to hold a market and fair, in the twelfth century. But even before this, it is likely that Preston's trade had been restricted to the burgesses – i.e. basically residents of the town who held some property – and that it was regulated through the framework of the Guild Merchant, perhaps from as early as Saxon times. The Preston Guild came to be held regularly every twenty years from 1562. Almost entirely ceremonial and social now, the Guild used to be very important to the economy of the area, 'enroling' the names of the burgesses of the borough who were allowed to trade freely without toll or hindrance. The town's system of government grew out of the old Guild Merchant. The reeve, or mayor, presided over the portmote, or borough court, and was helped by some of the principal burgesses and by other officials such as bailiffs, market lookers and the town clerk. This system survived more or less in this form until the Municipal Corporations Act of 1835.

At the same time, Preston was becoming an important legal and administrative centre, especially after Lancashire became a county in the twelfth century, and a county palatine shortly afterwards. The chancery court and perhaps also the exchequer of the palatine met in Preston. Later, the quarter sessions for Amounderness and Blackburn hundreds were held here, too, and even the Assizes were sometimes adjourned from the castle in Lancashire.

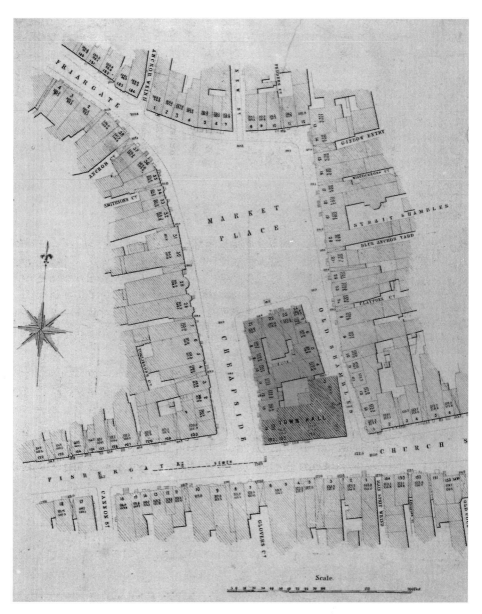

A plan of Preston market place about 150 years ago. Although the layout of the main streets – Fishergate, Church Street, Friargate – is the same today, practically nothing else is. The town hall shown on this plan was rebuilt shortly afterwards and itself burned down in 1947. Miller Arcade, the Harris Museum and Library, the Post Office building, the Sessions House and Town Hall on Birley Street all post-date this plan. Only here and there can glimpses of pre- Victorian Preston be seen: the narrow courts and yards running south from Church Street/Fishergate, and the odd place-name such as Anchor Court.

Preston was important. Even as early as 1087, when the survey for the Domesday Book was carried out, Preston was named as the main town in Amounderness: no fewer than 62 'vills' or hamlets were listed as being 'dependent' on it. And when the county was assessed for tax in 1218–19, Preston was the most wealthy town in the whole of Lancashire. Many thought that if Preston had only had a castle, it would have become the official county town in preference to Lancaster, which was smaller and much less accessible.

The Town and Guild Hall in 1727. From an engraving by S. and N. Buck.

In recognition of this, Preston was perhaps the first town in Lancashire to be 'incorporated' as a free borough by the granting of an official charter from the king. An early document known as the 'Costumal' lists the older privileges of the town, but the first definite grant was made by Henry II in about 1179. This was confirmed and extended at several times during the following centuries. The main effect was to give formal approval of the town's privilege to hold markets and fairs, and to make it more or less self-governing. Preston was also asked to send representatives to parliaments during the reign of Edward I, and we know that the town had MPs from 1295 until 1331, and again from 1529 onwards.

But it was not all peaceful growth and development during the Middle Ages. Life for most people was hard, insecure and uncertain. Warfare, fire, plague and famine could strike at any time, and there were no proper emergency services or insurance to lessen the blow. The Guild did its best to help individual members in trouble, and later, the county authorities did help with relief for plague and fire victims, but this was never enough. The worst period for Preston seems to have been the early fourteenth century, when natural calamities befell the town one after another.

A stone relief sculpture on the Town Hall, Birley Street: we know not of whom.

Political troubles during this period included the struggle for power between King Edward II and one of his greatest subjects, Thomas Earl of Lancaster – 'a sullen, envious, factious and quarrelsome man', nicknamed 'the old hog'. The Earl's demands for soldiers and money from Lancashire may have been a cause of the revolt in 1315

he Earl's right-hand man in the county, Sir
a band of men from the south-west of the
nd finally to Preston, which they captured.
under Sir Adam de Huddleston, but shortly
led by the sheriff of Lancashire at Deepdale,
and were soundly defeated.

ped the whole of England. It is difficult for
al the harvest was to life
ently. In medieval Eng-
e great hardship for the
om 1314 to 1316, three
price of grain, the staple
foodstuff, increased to about eight times its normal price!
These years almost certainly took their toll of life, and
left the town weakened and impoverished.

Then, in 1322, warfare returned to Preston, at the
hands of the Scots under Robert the Bruce. Just eight
years earlier the Scots under Bruce had finally reasserted
Scottish independence from England at Bannockburn.
Now, taking advantage of Edward II's weakness and pre-
occupation with the Earl of Lancaster, Bruce led a raid
over the border in June and marched with great speed

Preston had the great misfortune to lie on the main
road from Scotland. Robert
the Bruce was just one of
several Scottish visitors to
Preston.

through Carlisle and Lancaster, and on through Ellel, Wyresdale, Bleasdale
and the Fylde to Preston, raiding and looting as they went. There is a local
tradition that Preston was burned to the ground by the Scots, but we have
no solid proof of this – the town may have got off with just being sacked
and looted! Samlesbury and several other places south of the Ribble were
also raided before the Scots returned home after an entire operation which
took barely four weeks.

After all this, it is hardly surprising
that an 'inquisition' taken in 1341 found
widespread poverty and distress in Preston. And the worst was yet to come, for
only a generation after Bruce, the Black
Death – a terrible outbreak of bubonic
plague – swept through Europe. Starting
in central Asia, the disease reached Italy
in 1347, and England the following year.
In Preston at least one third of the entire

Fourteenth-century panel, showing
the burial of plague victims.

Preston parish church, 1796. This view is from the south, on Stoneygate. The church was originally dedicated to St Wilfrid, leading some to suppose that it was founded in the seventh century. Given the derivation of the place-name 'Priests' Town', this may just be accurate.

 Stoneygate was the main foot- and packhorse road south to the only bridge over the Ribble at Walton. The grammar school was on this road, as was the famous Cock Pit where Teetotalism was born. Richard Arkwright worked on his spinning frame in rooms at the back of the headmaster's house behind where the artist would have stood to draw this scene.

population – men, women and children – died of plague, mostly during the summer months. Three thousand in the parish of Preston died, and the total for the deanery of Amounderness as a whole was 13,180. There were recurrences of plague in 1361–62, 1369, and a very serious outbreak in 1630–31, as we shall see later.

# CHAPTER THREE

# *The Reformation and Tudor Preston*

AFTER the ravages of plague and economic dislocation, Preston did not really begin to expand again until well into the fifteenth century. At this time, the town still consisted of a few houses strung along the main streets – Fishergate, Friargate and Churchgate – and around the market place. The parish church, which was re-built and re-consecrated in 1581, was the focal point of the town. Around Preston, most of the forest had already been felled by the sixteenth century, and the town was surrounded by a patchwork system of small fields enclosed by hedges and ditches.

Throughout Europe at this time, there was growing dissatisfaction and

St George's Church is now the oldest surviving public building in use in Preston. It was built in 1724 as a chapel-of-ease to the parish church, but became a parish church in its own right in the middle of the last century. It is widely regarded by many as the most handsome Anglican church in town.

unrest about the way the Church was being run. There was a feeling that it had moved far away from the primitive simplicity and purity of the early Church and a powerful movement to reform it came into being. Henry VIII, though himself a Catholic, did much to weaken the old Church by ending the authority of the Pope in England and by closing down the monasteries. Lancashire did not have many great monasteries, but there were two minor houses in Preston. One was a hospital, dedicated to St Mary Magdalene, which stood in Maudlands near the present St Walburge's church. The other was a house of Franciscan friars which had been founded in 1221, just west of Friargate on Mount Pleasant; this property was sold to one Thomas Holcroft after it was closed down, and was used as a private residence for a time before becoming a House of Correction for the town, and, later, cottages.

St Mary's Catholic Church tucked behind Friargate, and built on a site right on the edge of the then town. In later, more tolerant times Catholic churches, such as St Wilfrid's (1793), St Augustine's (1840), English Martyrs (1867) and, particularly, Preston's 'cathedral', St Walburge's (1854) could all be built in much more prominent positions. St Mary's has now been demolished and is now (1997) a car park!

In central Lancashire, there was little direct opposition that we know about to the Dissolution of the Monasteries. Preston did not take part in the northern rebellion against the changes, the Pilgrimage of Grace, of 1536. But there was little enthusiasm for the new religion either, and many people retained strong sympathy for the old ways. Ever since that time Preston has had an influential Roman Catholic minority, considerably enlarged and strengthened by Catholic Irish immigration in the nineteenth century. The second church built in the town was a Catholic one, St Mary's in Friargate.

For a time, Protestants and Catholics lived side by side in Preston more or less happily. Divisions increased, however, as there developed, as in most other market towns, a body of opinion concerned that the Reformation had had little effect. Many thought that further reform was needed because, as one Richard Heyricke put it just before the Civil War:

> Popery has multiplied abundantly. In Lancashire it has superabounded above an hyperbole; the Mass has outfaced our Christian meetings, Jesuits have jeered our ministers, confronted and abused authority.

Strong feelings like these were to add considerable bitterness to the Civil War in the area.

During the Tudor years, the population increased, and a gradual price inflation brought economic opportunity to some, although certain social changes worried contemporaries. Preston began to take on the appearance of a prosperous, attractive and busy market town. From these years, too, date the beginnings of textile manufacture in Preston, with a small but increasingly important trade in wool and linen.

A lithograph of Preston parish church as it appeared before the latest rebuilding in the 1850s (it was said that the Anglican community had to respond to the building of the massively impressive new St Walburge's by commissioning a new, grander church of their own).

The original Preston settlement grew up around this site on the top of the bluff overlooking the Ribble; its commanding position led to its use as a lookout by soldiers in both the Civil War and the 1715 Rising.

# CHAPTER FOUR

# The Civil War and Stuart Preston

 N 1617 was made perhaps the first peaceful visit to Preston by a Scottish king. On his return from Scotland in August of that year, James VI and I stopped at various places in Lancashire including Preston, Myerscough, Hoghton (where, of course, the king reputedly dubbed the main course 'Sir Loin'), and the home of the Earls of Derby at Lathom House. A private diary of the time tells us: 'King came to Preston. There, at the Crosse, Mr Breres, the lawyer, made a Speeche and the Corporation presented him with a bowle; and then the King went to a banquet in the Town Hall.'

Preston has had several town halls. The hall where King James dined was mentioned in the royal charter of 1566 as 'a certain house within the said borough, vulgarly called the Toll-booth, otherwise the Moot-Hall'. In about 1684 local antiquarian Richard Kuerden said it was 'an ample ancient yet well beautifyed gylde or town hall or toll bothe, to which is annexed, at the end thereof, a counsell chamber'. In this hall, various law courts met, social functions were held, market tolls were levied and all kinds of public business was conducted. On the ground floor were butchers' shops. It stood – until it collapsed in 1780 – on Cheapside adjoining the market place and Fishergate.

Preston's position at the centre of the county meant that it had always been a very important market centre. At the end of the twelfth century, King John granted the town the right to hold an annual fair for eight days, but there must have been a thriving market well before this. By the seventeenth century there were regular markets every Wednesday, Friday and Saturday, and although the market place was 'so large . . . that few of the corporations of England exceed the same', it was overflowing. Most of the livestock was on display outside the main market, in Church Street and Fishergate. Swine were sold 'over against the church', causing a nuisance that was often complained about. There had also been a proposal to move the fish-stones to a smaller square which has now disappeared and become part of Lancaster Road.

The steady tempo of life in Preston was broken in 1630–31 by a serious outbreak of plague. The parish register notes ominously in November 1630:

'Heare beginith the Visitation of Almighty God the Plague', and the Guild order book of the same period states starkly that

> The great sickness of the plague of pestilence, wherein the number of eleven hundred persons dyed within the towne and parish of Preston, begann about the tenth day of November in anno 1630, and continued the space of one whole year next after.

The town was sealed off, food was hard to come by, and medical provision was hopelessly inadequate. After the outbreak, someone counted only 887 people left alive in the town, and of these 756 were receiving relief payments!

By comparison, the casualties and disturbance brought to Preston by the Civil Wars which broke out between Charles I and Parliament only a decade later were slight. In Lancashire, the wars consisted basically of a series of local engagements in which the important thing was to hold and control the major towns. The over-riding wish of most ordinary people was to avoid committing themselves to one side or the other, and to avoid the fighting, but in Preston the general inclination of most people, when they were forced to choose, was towards the king's cause.

Charles I. Most Prestonians, basically conservative then as now, were probably royalist in sympathy, but supported the parliamentarians when they had to. The king's hapless supporters at the Battle of Preston in 1648 were no match for the New Model Army under Oliver Cromwell.

Initially Preston was secured for the royalists by the mayor-elect Adam Morte, the high sheriff and a few others. They secured the magazine and defended the town with a double row of brick or mud walls. In February 1643 a parliamentarian army from the Manchester area attacked the town from the south and east. The fighting had raged for about two hours when one Captain Booth helped decide the outcome by climbing the outer wall and shouting to his men 'Follow me, or give me up for ever!' His bravery was matched on the royalist side by that of Adam Morte who

> had offentimes been heard sweare he would fire [i.e. burn down] the towne ere he gave it up, and beginne with his owne house . . . He came up to the souldiers very fearsly but was sleyn in a short space.

His death was a major loss to the royalist cause in Preston.

The parliamentarians took the town, but could not hold it for long. They strengthened the defences and guarded the 'Fryars Gate Barrs' strongly, but

A detail of Bucks' engraving of 1727 showing Walton Bridge, where the decisive stage of the Battle of Preston was fought in August 1648. Walton Flats, site of the ancient Roman station, together with the meandering River Darwen, can be seen in the foreground.

when the Earl of Derby approached with some royalists in March the garrison melted away, 'for the Townsmen were generally disaffected to the Parliament'. The town changed hands once again not long after, when the royalists had lost their grip on the rest of Lancashire.

It was Preston's misfortune, as we have seen already, to lie on the main road south from Scotland. Barely two years after Charles I had lost the First Civil War, a Scottish army led by the Duke of Hamilton invaded England to restore him to the throne. Some English royalists under Sir Marmaduke Langdale, a veteran Scots army under George Munro, and several smaller units joined in. Together, the invading force numbered some 20,000. Opposing them for parliament, Oliver Cromwell and his able lieutenant John Lambert had barely 9,000 men from the New Model Army and the Lancashire militia.

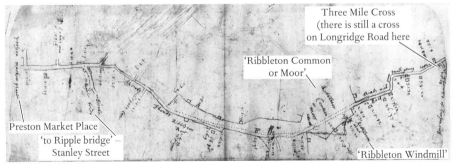

Three Mile Cross (there is still a cross on Longridge Road here

'Ribbleton Common or Moor'.

Preston Market Place
'to Ripple bridge' –
Stanley Street

'Ribbleton Windmill'

A remarkable late seventeenth-century manuscript map showing the main road to Longridge from Preston Market Place to Three Mile Cross at Grimsargh. One crucial feature allows us to place the beginning of the Battle of Preston with confidence, for one parliamentarian report of the battle speaks of Cromwell's men coming into contact with the royalists at Ribbleton Windmill. The road is not properly made up and is lined with shrubs and small trees. Cromwell bemoaned the boggy ground and the small fields which made it difficult for his men to fight.

The scene was set for a remarkable and historic confrontation. On 17 August 1648 Preston secured its place in national history books, for although the Battle of Preston is little remembered locally (the site is not marked on the ground in any way) and it is sometimes confused with the Jacobite incursions of 1715 or 1745, the battle was in fact crucial to the whole historical and political development of the country. If the royalists won, Charles I was to be restored to the throne to rule in a more authoritarian way then ever before. But the parliamentarian army had already resolved that if they won the campaign, the king would be put on trial for treason for having

Oliver Cromwell, whose chance to become Lord Protector was earned at Preston.

re-started the civil wars and, crime of crimes, for having invited a Scottish army to invade England!

The Duke of Hamilton was a brave man but a poor commander. On the march south, he had failed to keep his disparate army and squabbling commanders together. On the eve of battle, his cavalry was near Wigan while most of the infantry was still at Preston, and many of his best troops were way back at Lancaster. Their eastern flank was guarded by the small unit of Marmaduke Langdale, who spent the night of the 16th somewhere near Longridge. With all his men Cromwell had marched with great speed from South

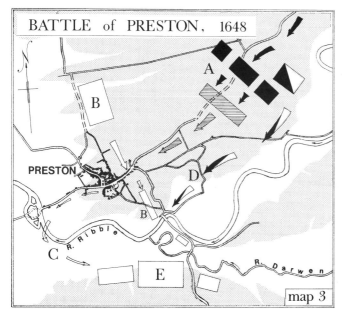

The narrow lane to Fishwick Bottoms down which the Lancashire regiments made their way to Walton Bridge to engage the Scots 'at push of pike'.

Wales, via Yorkshire, and camped that same night at Stonyhurst. Early on the morning of the battle, unbeknown to the royalists, Cromwell's forces marched down the north bank of the Ribble and surprised Langdale's men at Ribbleton (see map 3A). Hamilton refused to believe that Cromwell's whole force had attacked, and he was persuaded by his wilful second-in-command, the Earl of Callendar, to continue moving his infantry from Preston moor, across the bridge at Walton-le-Dale, to the south bank of the river (B).

Langdale fought a desperate and gallant action with pike and musket in the fields and lanes to the east of Preston but, without help from the Scots, he could not hold out and was eventually forced back into the town. Hamilton tried bravely to save the situation by rallying a handful of men at the end of Church Street but personal valour could not correct his strategic and tactical errors; he had to pull back and could only re-join his infantry south of the Ribble by swimming across the swollen river west of the town (C).

Meanwhile, the Lancashire regiments, which Cromwell had wisely kept in reserve took advantage of an unguarded lane down to the bridge (D, *and photograph, above*), and fought a bloody engagement 'at push of pike' before managing to clear the bridge of its Scottish defenders. Before nightfall, Cromwell had also taken the Darwen bridge, and had come within musket shot of the enemy on Cinnamon Hill (E). Most of the Scots had taken no part in the battle at all, but were so disheartened and badly prepared for another fight that they retreated south in a drumless march that night.

Preston had been a bloody battle: most of it consisted of close hand-to-hand fighting in confined terrain, and many hundreds were killed or wounded, although the town itself seems to have missed out on the worst effects of the battle. The campaign was not yet over, but its outcome had been decided at Preston. Charles I was executed on 30 January 1649, and a republic was established shortly afterwards. Cromwell himself became Lord Protector in 1653.

These years were relatively peaceful and prosperous, but most Prestonians

Cattermole's rather fanciful depiction of the climax of the fighting at Walton Bridge on 17 August 1648, Preston's biggest day in history so far.

retained a strong sympathy for the monarchy. Charles II had actually been proclaimed king at the market cross in the town in July 1649, and when he was finally and properly restored in 1660, there was great rejoicing in the streets of Preston. The bells of the parish church rang for three days!

# CHAPTER FIVE

# Proud Preston: The Eighteenth Century

N 1715, within living memory of that bloody battle between Cromwell and Hamilton, another Scottish army came south intending to restore a Stuart king. Again, the outcome was decided at Preston. By this time, the last Stuart king, James II, had been replaced by Protestant monarchs, but in Scotland and parts of England many people sought the return of the old line. A rebellion broke out in favour of the Old Pretender (or James III), and in November 1715 one army of rebels marched into Preston on its way south. The town welcomed the Jacobite army – a 'gallant gentlemanly army' – and James was proclaimed king at the market cross. Within a few days, however, an army loyal to George I, and led by one General Wills, had gathered enough

Plan of the 1715 Battle. As well as the disposition of forces, the ford over Penwortham Holme is clearly visible, as is Walton Bridge and the principal features of the town.

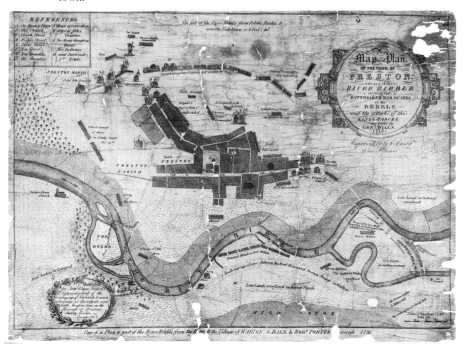

strength to attack the rebels in Preston. The Scots erected barricades at the ends of the main streets and succeeded in fighting off one attack. But they realised that their cause was not going to attract popular support in England and they surrendered, despite their initial victory. Among the reasons given for their failure, the most colourful was that: 'The Ladys in this toune, Preston, are so beautifull & so richly attired, that the Gentlemen Soldiers . . . minded nothing but courting and feasting' during their days in Preston!

No better fortune attended yet another Stuart pretender, Charles Edward, when he invaded a generation later. Bonny Prince Charlie did not stay long in Preston, but he greatly admired the view from Avenham Walks as he contemplated the sad fate of previous ventures. It was said that 'he received the greatest emotions on this enchanting spot'.

By this date, taking the air on Avenham Walks had become a favourite social pastime for the locals. The area had been bought by the Corporation in 1696 and laid out with trees in the way we see it in Buck's famous engraving.

A section of Yates' Map of Lancashire of 1786. Preston was just about to undergo a complete transformation, as the arrival of industry and the massive increase in population it brought changed the size, appearance and character of the town for ever. By this date Penwortham (Old) Bridge had been built. Note the race tracks on both Fulwood and Preston moors.

Detail of Bucks' 'South View of Preston'.
Avenham Walks are seen clearly, complete with
pedestrians. Patten House (no. 9) and the parish
church are also shown.

On visiting the town in 1727, Daniel Defoe commented that the Walks 'command one of the most delectable scenes in England. No lover of nature can survey it without transport.'

In fact, few people came to Preston without remarking favourably about the town. They praised its position on 'a clean delightful eminence', and also the town's 'beautiful aspect'. Lady Oxford wrote that Preston was 'a very clean pleasant town consisting of two large streets wherein many of the neighbouring gentry have good winter houses'. It was 'one of the prettiest retirements in England, and may for its beauty and largeness compare with most cities, and for the politeness of the inhabitants none can excel. It is vulgarly called *Proud Preston* on account of its being a place of the best fashion'.

And so it was! Many rich and landed families had taken up residence in Preston, and as one visitor noted: 'Among the Lancashire towns, Preston is that which had always taken the lead in the point of gentility'. Being the administrative centre of the county, Preston attracted many lawyers, clerks and other professionals. Besides, Preston was undoubtedly a very pleasant place to live. Rich patrons like the Lawes, Pattens, Wilsons and Winckleys provided work for a large number of other people – craftsmen, artists, suppliers of luxury goods and especially domestic servants and lawyers.

Taking the air on Avenham Walks in the early
nineteenth century. Polite society in the smartest
part of town.

Preston became a favourite social resort, especially during the winter when the social life for the rich was spectacular and exciting. Balls, parties and assemblies were held in the great houses and in the town hall. For some, entertainment centred on organisations like the oddly named 'Oyster and Parched Pea Club' which met in the town's most famous tavern, the Mitre Inn on the market place, and the 'Walton Mock Corporation' which was suspected of being a front for political activity, but whose aims appear to have been purely social.

The Preston Guild, held every twenty years, was always the high point of the social calendar, as indeed it still remains. By the eighteenth century, the Guild had lost most of its original importance, but more and more time and money were spent on its social functions. The most opulent was the one held in 1822, just before the Derby family left the town for good, and before the arrival of industry changed irrevocably the character of the town.

Preston's buildings were greatly praised. 'The generality of the buildings, especially in 2 or 3 of the great streets, were very handsome, better than in most county towns'. Patten House, built by the barrister Thomas Patten, was particularly grand. It stood on Church Street, nearly opposite the church,

The highlight of the social calendar was Preston Guild. The last of the old, pre-industrial Guilds was that held in 1822. Such was the social and cultural change in the town over the next generation that there was a serious debate as to whether the 1842 Guild should be held at all. Horse-racing was held at various times on Preston and Fulwood Moors and also on Penwortham Holme.

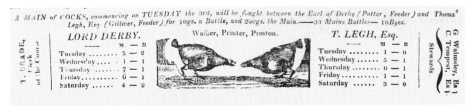

An advertisement for a cock-fight between the birds of Lord Derby and T. Legh Esq., to be held at the Guild of 1822.

Preston Town Hall, built in 1782 after the previous one had fallen down (Preston has been perhaps uniquely unlucky with its municipal buildings). It was demolished in 1860 when it was decided to built a new Hall more in keeping with the town's new-found wealth and civic pride.

and came to belong to the Stanleys after Patten's daughter married into that family. Originally built of stone, it was refaced in brick in 1721 when that material came into fashion. Richard Kuerden wrote in about 1684: 'The streets belonging to this town or borough are very spacious, good handsome buildings on either side, here and there interwoven with stately fabrics of brickbuilding after the Modish manner, extraordinarily adorning the streets which they belong unto'. It was perhaps a sign of the changing times when Patten House was pulled down in 1835.

Naturally, the town was not all gaiety and light. The number of people who shared in the opulence and wealth of Preston was very small, and very few people lived in homes like Patten House. For most people there was no running water, no adequate sanitation and few luxuries. There was considerable poverty and distress in many of the narrow streets behind the smart façades of Fishergate and Church

Street. Yet, relative both to other towns of the period, and to what Preston itself was like a generation later, Preston at the end of the eighteenth century was smart, wealthy, clean and proud – 'The Lancashire Capua' was one description.

Old Penwortham Bridge (1759), the second bridge across the Ribble. The old Southport railway line, whose station was near the bottom of Fishergate Hill, crossed the river by means of a bridge just a few yards upstream (the Penwortham by-pass now follows the line of this former railway up to Cop Lane and beyond).

# CHAPTER SIX

# Change and Growth: Nineteenth-Century Preston

HIS SECTION of the present History takes us up to the end of the last century. It looks at both the physical growth and development of the town, and also at the social and economic fortunes of its people. At first sight, Preston in 1850 is a world apart from the Preston of fifty years earlier, and in many ways, of course, this impression is fully justified. Beneath this exterior, however, many features did remain unchanged or at least recognisable, and it would be foolish to imagine that everything was swept aside by the arrival of industry.

One thing that did not change very quickly was the appalling state of the roads. Most seem to have been rough dirt tracks, almost impassable in winter. The Preston–Wigan road, for example, was very busy and important, and had been turnpiked very early, in 1726, but this is what Arthur Young had to say about it later in the century:

> I know not in the whole range of language terms sufficiently expressive to describe this infernal highway . . . Let me seriously caution all travellers who may accidentally purpose to travel this terrible country, to avoid it as they would the devil!

And he claimed to have found ruts four feet deep! Things did get better

The Old Tram Bridge across the Ribble. The tramroad connected the Lancaster Canal to the Leeds & Liverpool at Walton Summit (the cost of building locks and an aqueduct across the Ribble and its valley were too great for a navigable link to be built). Today the Lancaster Canal stops just short of where it used to cross the significantly named Aqueduct Street. Traces of its route into town can still be seen on Fylde Road (near the Watering Trough pub) and behind Leighton Street. The canal terminus was beside the Corn Exchange (later the Public Hall and now the Corn Exchange again).

slowly and coach services increased rapidly during the 1770s. Both Fishergate Hill and London Road were re-built and had their inclines reduced. Penwortham Bridge (now 'Old Penwortham Bridge') was built in 1759 (an earlier one having fallen down just after completion) to carry the main Liverpool road. The oldest bridge crossing in the area, Walton bridge, was re-built in 1782, and a new one was built at Brockholes Brow (at the 'Tickled Trout') in 1824 for the new Blackburn turnpike.

In 1798 the Lancaster Canal was opened. Five years later, it was connected by a horse-drawn tramroad to the Leeds and Liverpool Canal extension at Walton summit. Used until the 1860s, mainly to bring coal from south Lancashire, the tramroad ran from the end of the Lancaster Canal near the Corn Exchange on Wharf Street, and tunnelled under Fishergate – amazingly there is still a tunnel on the site, now giving access to the Fishergate Centre car park from Charnley Street – and on to the corner of Ribblesdale Place from where its route can still be followed through Avanham Park to the top of the steep slope above the 'Old Tram Bridge'. Tubs of coal were pulled up this slope by a steam-operated winding engine on the site of the present Belvedere, which was moved to this spot from Miller Park to make room for the statue of the Earl of Derby.

The first public square outside London to be lit by gas: the Obelisk carried a 22″ lamp. The stumpy clock tower of the Town Hall can just be seen on the left.

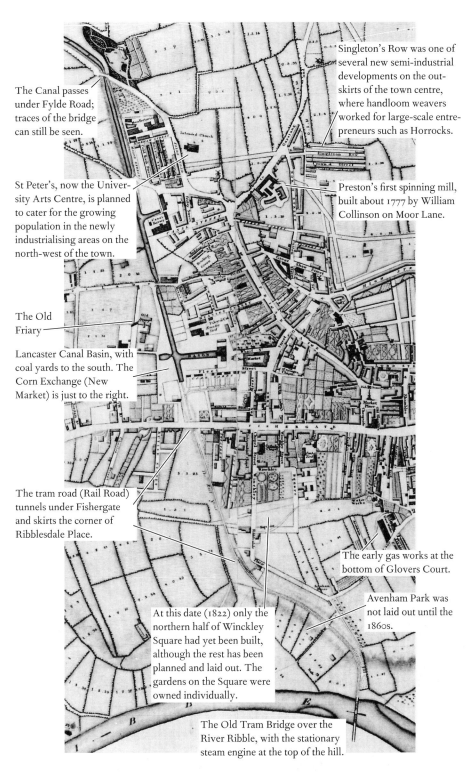

The Canal passes under Fylde Road; traces of the bridge can still be seen.

Singleton's Row was one of several new semi-industrial developments on the outskirts of the town centre, where handloom weavers worked for large-scale entrepreneurs such as Horrocks.

St Peter's, now the University Arts Centre, is planned to cater for the growing population in the newly industrialising areas on the north-west of the town.

Preston's first spinning mill, built about 1777 by William Collinson on Moor Lane.

The Old Friary

Lancaster Canal Basin, with coal yards to the south. The Corn Exchange (New Market) is just to the right.

The tram road (Rail Road) tunnels under Fishergate and skirts the corner of Ribblesdale Place.

The early gas works at the bottom of Glovers Court.

Avenham Park was not laid out until the 1860s.

At this date (1822) only the northern half of Winckley Square had yet been built, although the rest has been planned and laid out. The gardens on the Square were owned individually.

The Old Tram Bridge over the River Ribble, with the stationary steam engine at the top of the hill.

A section of Shakeshaft's map of 1822, showing part of the town centre.

Preston was the first provincial town to have gas street lighting. In May 1815, only about a year after parts of London had been lit, the Preston Gas Light Company held its first meeting. Money was raised and one Mr Grafton was commissioned as engineer to erect lights along parts of Church Street, Fishergate and the top of Friargate. Grafton did not miss much, and he tried to save money where he could: instead of using cast-iron pipes, he bought a supply of army-surplus musket barrels from Birmingham, and used them, stuck end to end, to carry the gas in some of the sections! Needless to say, there were so many leaks that the whole thing had to be put right the year after. The Gas Company's other claim to fame was the illumination of the market place from a 22″ gas light at the top of the Obelisk in 1816. It was fitting that when this Obelisk was returned to the Square in 1979, on the occasion of the borough's octocentenary, an electric light was placed at the top.

One of the main reasons for the interest in gas lighting was its possible use in illuminating the mills so that longer hours could be worked. By this time, the cotton trade in Preston had really begun to expand and provide a spur to the rest of the town's economy. There had actually been a textile trade on a small scale in the town since at least the sixteenth century. At first it was not cotton, but wool and linen, which formed the basis of this trade.

Both flax and hemp were grown in west Lancashire, though most supplies came from Ireland via the port at Preston. The burgess roll of 1562 showed a large increase in the number of residents who classed themselves as flax sellers or weavers. As someone noted in 1705, 'The making of linen cloth hath, for many ages been the settled trade [there] . . . and is the sole dependence of thousands of families'. But in 1727 Preston was said to be 'beyond the trading part of the county', and the real growth as a textile centre did not take place until much later.

Handloom weaving was a hugely important part of the early industrial economy throughout central Lancashire. Thousands of families worked together supplying merchants and entrepreneurs. Youngsters and wives were kept busy with spinning and ancillary operations, while the husband sat at the handloom, often in damp cellars (in order to keep the yarn moist) or ground-floor loom-shops. When power weaving was gradually introduced in factories, wages for handloom weavers fell dramatically and many hundreds migrated into Preston and other towns from the surrounding countryside to look for work.

In 1732 Richard Arkwright was born in Preston, the youngest son of a poor family. While staying in Arkwright House in Stoneygate in 1768, he applied for a patent for the new machine he had developed. His 'spinning frame' overcame a major technical problem – how to spin cotton yarn mechanically using water or horse power, and therefore cheaply and efficiently. Arkwright himself achieved fame and great wealth from his invention and its application helped enormously in the mechanisation of the cotton industry.

The other man whose name is closely associated with the early history of cotton manufacture in Preston was John Horrocks (no relation apparently to that renowned Prestonian of the seventeenth century, Jeremiah Horrocks, who was one of the world's first observational astronomers). John Horrocks was born in Edgworth near Bolton and came to Preston in 1786 where, 'taking advantage of the important improvements then introduced in the art of cotton

(*Above*) Arkwright House and, in the distance, the parish church which stands at the top of Stoneygate. It was in rooms at the rear of Arkwright House that Richard Arkwright worked on the design for his patented water frame (*top right*), the first practicable mechanised cotton spinning machine. Prior to this, it had taken many spinners to keep a handloom weaver busy, and the mechanisation of spinning led to a huge boom in the cotton trade, central to Preston's nineteenth-century industrialisation. Yet Arkwright did not instigate or even contribute directly to the Industrial Revolution in the town: it was pure coincidence that he happened to be in Preston while he was working on his invention.

spinning', he opened several mills. His 'Yellow Factory', so called because it was painted on the outside with a yellow wash, was opened in 1791, and was quickly followed by others, at the east end of Church Street, by the canal, and at the bottom of Turk's Head Court. Horrocks's mills were not the first in Preston – the earliest had been opened in 1777 by Messrs Collinson & Watson – but Horrocks was responsible, more than anyone else, for establishing the town as a major textile centre. A song supporting his campaign for election to parliament in 1796 claimed, not without justification:

> When Horrocks first to Preston came
> How great a blessing reached the town,
> To him the town ascribes its trade
> The poor shall bless his favoured name . . .

Near the site of the modern factory, north of New Hall Lane, Horrocks & Co. also owned several hand-loom weaving sheds. With the gradual introduction of efficient power looms and of steam engines to drive them, there was less demand for the work of the hand-loom weavers. But it would be wrong to assume that they disappeared, victims of the new technology.

In 1816, the Horrocks's still 'employed a whole countryside of weavers' to whom work was 'put out'. And even in the 1850s most cotton firms regularly gave work to non-mechanised, small manufacturers, mainly because this allowed them to respond more quickly to market fluctuations. Rather than take on extra workers in the mills for short periods, they put work out to the small producers. Wages for the hand-loom weavers dropped alarmingly, though, and many families were left without a living – some hand-loom weavers saw their wages fall from 16s. 3d. a week to only 6s. 6d.! In 1836 John Lennon was right in saying that the time was 'gone past, gone for ever, when it

The Yellow Factory.                     would be prudent for men to

A 'General View of Preston' at the turn of the century. On the left is the East Lancashire railway. Originally this ran to its own terminus in what is now the Fishergate Centre car park, cutting between Avenham and Miller Parks by way of a splendid skew-arched bridge (still there). The Borough Council even obliged the railway company to construct a footpath on its river bridge (still there). Originally the embankment carrying this line across the flood plain south of the river was a viaduct, but it was later filled in to make the embankment we see here. The pedestrians in the foreground are walking along the Old Tram Road, which had closed some 40 years earlier. Just look at the chimneys on the skyline!

depend on handloom weaving as a safe means of procuring a decent livelihood'. There were jobs in the new mills that were springing up, but many weavers were too proud to take them, at least at first.

By 1825 there were forty-one cotton mills in Preston. Then, in the 1840s, a lot more were built in a short time, mainly because capital was freer and because the railways brought cheaper coal. In 1844 'the town was increasing at a very rapid rate, tall chimneys and loom-sheds were rising as if by magic'. As in the other towns on the north of the Lancashire 'cotton belt', weaving was the main manufacturing process that went on in the new mills, but there was spinning too, and from about the 1830s nearly all the new mills that were built combined both operations in the same factory. The Preston area, like Clitheroe, was famous for its high-quality light cloths made from fine yarns.

Most vacancies in the new mills were filled by 'immigrant' labour from the surrounding countryside and from further afield. The town's Irish (and Roman Catholic) community increased substantially in the later 1840s because of the Potato Famine in Ireland. The native population in Preston also increased. Therefore, from a level that had remained roughly constant at about 6,000 for most of the eighteenth century, the population of Preston

Starkie's Iron and Wire Mills, from a trade directory, *c.* 1890. The main part of the building is still standing, recently renovated, in Cotton Court, just to the south of Church Street.

just about doubled every twenty years until it had reached 83,000 by 1861! Thereafter, the rate of increase slackened off.

The 1851 census shows that more than 18,000 Prestonians worked in the cotton trade – a staggering 48–50% of the entire working population. For much of the century, cotton was supreme, and was the mainspring of the town's economy. There were other industries and employers, of course. The second

The recently renovated Corn Exchange. For most Prestonians, however, this is the front of the Public Hall, where Franz Liszt played and many famous events, balls and concerts took place over the years. The concert hall, with one of the best dance floors in the north of England, extended well back towards Corporation Street on the left of the picture. The death knell for the Public Hall was sounded when plans for Preston Ringway were passed. The present Guild Hall was commissioned for the 1972 Guild and for 20 years, until the recent completion of the Penwortham By-pass, the dual carriageway actually went around both sides of the building! The Public Hall was a great loss to the town.

most numerous group was usually the domestic servants, followed by labourers, boot and shoe makers and dressmakers. There was also a healthy engineering industry in Preston, which stood the town in good stead when cotton began to decline at the turn of the century and after. There were several foundries, coal yards and builders' yards. And it should be remembered that in 1822 a Corn Exchange, not a Cotton Exchange, was built at the bottom of Lune Street, by the canal basin.

One reason that was given why Preston's trade was not dominated by cotton to so great an extent as in other Lancashire towns was its poor labour-relations record. Certainly there were several damaging strikes and disputes – over low and falling wages, the introduction of machinery, and occasionally because of political agitation. The

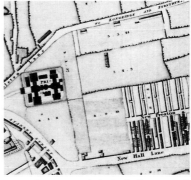

A small section of Shakeshaft's map of Preston, showing Preston Prison on the left and, on the right, the new rows of terraces being laid out along New Hall Lane. This is now the site of the Centenary Works. St Mary's Street has yet to be built connecting New Hall Lane and Ribbleton Lane.

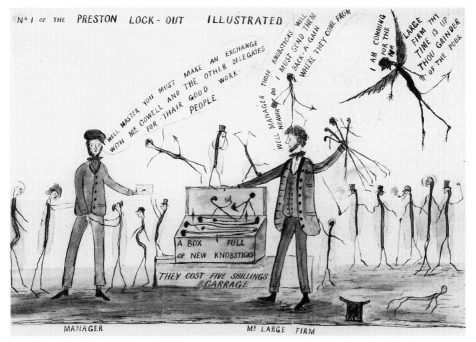

A cartoon from the time of the Preston Lock-out showing the cotton masters taking blackleg workers – 'knobsticks' – from a box. Note, top right, the avenging angel announcing 'I am coming for the Mr Large Firm, thy time is up, thou grinder of the poor'. Perhaps Dickens had heard of the Preston cotton masters' reputation when, in *Hard Times*, he characterised Mr Gradgrind as the unfeeling exploiter of the poor.

# THE COTTON LORDS
## OF PRESTON.

Have you not heard the news of late,
About some mighty men so great,
I mean the swells of Fishergate,
  The Cotton Lords of Preston.
They are a set of stingy Blades,
They've lock'd up all their Mills and
  Shades,
So now we've nothing else to do,
But come a singing songs for you,
So with our ballads we've come out,
To tramp the country round about,
And try if we cannot live without
  The Cotton Lords of Preston.

### CHORUS.

Everybody's crying shame,
On these Gentlemen by name;
Dont you think they're much to blame
  The Cotton Lords of Preston.

The working people such as we,
Pass their time in misery,
While they live in luxury,
  The Cotton Lords of Preston.
They're making money every way,
And building Factories every day,
Yet when we ask them for more pay,
They had the impudence to say,
To your demands we'll not consent,
You get enough so be content,

But we will have the Ten per Cent,
  From the Cotton Lords of Preston,
   Everybody's crying shame&c.

Our Masters say they're very sure,
That a strike we can't endure,
They all assert we're very poor.
  The Cotton Lords of Preston.
But we've determined every one,
With them we'll not be done,
For we'll not be content,
Until we get the Ten per Cent,
The Cotton Lords are sure to fall,
Both ugly, handsome, short and tall,
For we intend to conquer all,
  The Cotton Lords of Preston.
   Everybod's crying shame &c.

So men and women all of you,
Come and buy a song or two,
And assist us to subdue,
  The Cotton Lords of Preston,
We'll conquer them and no mistake,
Whatever Laws they seem to make,
And when we get the Ten per Cent,
Then we'll live happy and content,
O then we'll dance and sing with glee,
And thank you all right heartily,
When we gain the victory,
And beat the Lords of Preston.
   Everybody's crying shame &c.

A fund-raising song-sheet dating from the Preston Lock-out.

A section of the First Edition Ordnance Survey map showing the town centre.

Winckley Square from Ribblesdale Place, with Chapel Street in the distance. Some of the richest families lived on this, one of the most handsome early nineteenth-century squares in the country.

In 1868 this impressive building opened its doors for the first time: the Preston Union Workhouse on Watling Street Road. One wonders what the householders across the road thought of their new neighbours, for in the 1850s cottages and villas had begun to be built in Fulwood Park, a Freehold Land Society estate centring on Victoria Road and Lower Bank Road.

The Workhouse changed its name just after the Second World War to the Civic Hostel (!) and finally closed in 1979. The building has become the headquarters of the local regional health authority. But why only sand-blast the bit in the middle?

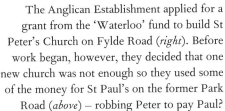

The Anglican Establishment applied for a grant from the 'Waterloo' fund to build St Peter's Church on Fylde Road (*right*). Before work began, however, they decided that one new church was not enough so they used some of the money for St Paul's on the former Park Road (*above*) – robbing Peter to pay Paul?

first spinners' union was formed in 1836 during a strike, and in 1842 five operatives were killed by the soldiers the owners had nervously called in (an event recently commemorated by a specially commissioned sculpture outside the Corn Exchange). Wages dropped again, by 10 per cent, in 1847, and when they had not returned to their previous level when trade improved in 1853, both the spinners and the less well organised weavers struck:

> In eighteen forty-seven, my boys
> I am sorry for to say
> They took from us the ten per cent,
> Without so much delay
> And now we want it back again,
> Our masters in a pout
> Said they would not grant it us,
> So we're everyone locked out . . .

The dispute dragged on for nearly a whole year, and became a struggle of attrition. After a time, the issue went beyond mere wages. In September, shortly before the lock-out began, Thomas Miller, the richest man in Preston, and leader of the Masters' Association said that 'Mastery, not wages, was now the central issue'. And the weavers' leader, George Cowell, also saw it in wider terms – as a struggle against 'the tyranny of the cotton lords', whom

The Central Methodist Chapel on Lune Street, viewed from the top of St George's Shopping Centre car park. County Hall is at top right; Fishergate Baptist Church is at top left.

he likened to 'the slaveholders of the United States of America'. The owners particularly objected to the unions' move to collect a subscription from the men whose employers had granted the 10%, in order to help those who were still on strike. This provoked the Masters' Association to impose a general lock-out, and to resolve that any of their members who gave in to the workers' demands should be fined £5,000. After the worst winter for forty years, the employers started to use blackleg labour – knobsticks – and the strike collapsed shortly after the workers' leaders were arrested in March 1854. It is not surprising that during the American Civil War the sympathies of the workers lay with Lincoln and the North, despite the hardships caused during the so-called 'Cotton Famine'.

In 1768, after the Preston parliamentary election, the Whigs, led by the Stanleys, made an appeal to the House of Commons, and managed to get the House to agree to their contention that every male inhabitant over 21 had the vote in Preston. This ruling gave Preston the widest franchise of any borough in the country until the Reform Act of 1832 standardised the qualification. The result was very hectic, exciting and violent elections. It also drew in many Radical candidates to fight them, including Joseph Hanson, Dr Crompton, William Cobbett and, in 1830, Henry Hunt. Hunt, 'the Orator', had been the speaker at St Peter's Fields in Manchester in 1819 when the famous 'Peterloo Massacre' occurred. In December 1830 he surprised everyone – including, it was said, himself – when he won a turbulent by-election in Preston. Many people in the town were deeply concerned at his victory because it had been obvious to everyone that his chief support had come from the 'lower orders', or the 'working classes' as they were increasingly called. This demonstration of the political influence of Radicalism and of popular movements worried Whigs and Tories alike. The Earl of Derby moved away from Preston shortly afterwards, partly because of his defeat in the poll, and partly because of the industrialisation of the town.

What the election also showed were the social divisions in the town. Most of the high classes kept 'a respectable distance' from their social inferiors. As Whittle noted in his *History* in 1837, 'a regular distance is always kept between the various ranks of society; inferiority is often met, in the public walks, with repulsive countenance and half-averted eyes'. In many ways, this was an inevitable consequence of increasing segregation of the classes into different housing in different parts of the town. At first, hundreds of tiny dwellings had been crammed into the existing parts of Preston, behind the old houses on the main streets and in courtyards. But gradually new houses were built on the outskirts of the town where the new mills were opening – by the canal, to the north and to the east in 'New Preston'. For the middle and upper classes, on the other hand, smart new suburbs grew up away from the smoke and dirt of the factories (i.e. upwind of them), in Avenham, around Winckley Square, Ribblesdale Place and Bushell Place. Later still, towards the end of the nineteenth century and afterwards, the working-class areas spread further and further outwards beyond the old borough boundaries until they met the new middle-class suburbs of Ashton and Fulwood.

Most of the new working-class houses were, of course, built in terraces. Really just rows of traditional cottages joined together, they were erected back to back, either physically or, more usually, separated by back yards, with or without back streets as well. In 1844, even after a huge new reservoir had

Preston houses, from a *Report on the Sanitary Conditions in Preston* by Rev. John Clay, 1842, in which he talks of the 'miasmata generated in filth and putridity'. Note the open cesspool between the back yards. The early industrial communities of factory and houses were often built on the edge of town like this, later to be surrounded by more and more development.

Some terraces are architecturally uniform, but others, such as these on Roebuck Street, betray their origins as really no more than a series of cottages built alongside each other.

been built at Grimsargh, about 70 per cent of the houses in Preston were not supplied with running water. Without water closets or inside toilets, these houses were appallingly unhealthy. There was usually a 'privy', cess pit or ash pit in the back yard, which was cleaned out by 'scavengers' irregularly and infrequently. Sewers were not begun to be built on a wide scale until the 1850s, and it took a long time to complete the system. Cholera and typhus were rampant, and infant mortality was frighteningly high among working-class families. In this regard, certainly at the end of the century, Preston had the worst record of any town in England.

Of course, people had been living without adequate sanitation for centuries, but the cramped conditions, the overcrowding and the general poverty and harshness of life for most people during the decades of early industrialisation meant that average life expectancy actually dropped markedly, from about 31 years in the 1780s, to just 23 in 1831. The main problem was with sanitation and those filthy back yards where, as Charles Dickens said in *Hard Times* (in which his fictional Coketown was based on Preston in the 1840s), 'Nature was as strongly bricked out as killing airs and gases were bricked in'. 'Improvers' like the architect James Hibbert, the local surveyor Henry Wrigg and Joseph Livesey, together with the Local Board of Health which from 1874 was led by the meticulous Dr Pilkington, waged a campaign to get stricter building regulations for the new housing, and for healthier conditions generally. It was a slow task, and it met with resistance, but things did gradually improve.

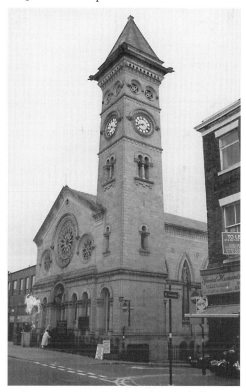

On 31 October 1838 the Preston–Wigan railway was opened. There had been those

Fishergate Baptist Church – along with the Harris Museum and St James' Church on Aven-ham Lane (demolished in the early 1980s), the best work of Preston architect and 'Improver', James Hibbert.

who were sceptical, like the man who had written to the Editor of the *Preston Pilot* in 1825,

> Sir . . . I think gullibility's self can hardly believe that a carriage can, by a locomotive engine, move, even upon a newly constructed railway, at the rate of ten or twelve miles per hour; those who can believe this might, with equally reasoned arguments, be persuaded that it is possible to ride through the air on a broomstick!

The bridge in the foreground is the East Lancashire railway bridge (just visible to the left of the tree are the stairs carrying the footpath up on to the deck of the bridge. Beyond is the magnificent North Union railway bridge, which was built in 1838 to carry the Preston–Wigan line (now the main west-coast rail line). The bridge has since been widened.

But the North Union trains from Wigan soon proved that they could go as fast as 30 m.p.h. Within three years, other lines had been opened to Lancaster,

Longridge (used mainly to carry building stone from the quarries there), and Fleetwood. Branch lines were built to Blackpool and Lytham, and the East Lancashire line was completed when their new bridge was built across the Ribble (between the main railway line and the Old Tram Bridge) in 1850.

In the early days, there were no fewer than three main-line stations in Preston and arguments between the railway companies helped give the Lancaster Canal a new lease of life. Fast packet boats carried passengers to and from Lancaster in relative luxury – refreshments were served on board and the boats were even heated in winter. The Water Witch completed the journey in just three and a half hours, and cost only 1s. 6d. for a first-class ticket, which compared with a whole 5 shillings on the train. This competition worried the railway directors greatly, and in 1842 they took the very unusual step of leasing their railway to the Canal Company for 21 years. The speed of the trains was crucial in the end,

The North Union railway bridge around the turn of the century.

however, and the railway cancelled the lease. The arrival of the railways brought to the ordinary people of Preston the chance to get away for the day, or for a longer break, and the cheap trains to Fleetwood and Blackpool were enormously popular.

With the huge expansion of the town, many new churches were built. By 1852 there were ten Anglican churches in Preston, and five Roman Catholic. The grandest of the latter was St Walburge's, the work of the designer of the Hansom cab, Joseph Hansom. Its magnificent spire, built partly from old stone railway sleepers, still dominates Preston's skyline from every direction. It was said that the grandeur of this church shamed the Anglican establishment into re-building the parish church, St John's, even though it had been re-built as recently as 1770, and had been given a new tower in only 1813–14. The strength and

St John the Divine, Preston. This structure dates from 1855, but the site it occupies has been a Christian site for over 1,000 years.

An aerial photograph of Preston showing row upon row of terraced housing, apparently interrupted only by industrial buildings and mills. New Hall Lane is the road running from the bottom right-hand corner (St Matthew's Church is the large building in the corner. The Centenary Mill is on the left, with the star-shaped buildings of the prison just beyond.

vitality of Catholicism in the town tended to make support for the nonconformist churches that much weaker, although John Wesley preached to 'a very serious congregation' in Preston in 1781 and 1784, and there was no shortage of different groups. The Methodist Sunday schools were usually better attended than any of the other educational establishments in the town –

whether the old Free Grammar School or the National School that was set up for the children of poor families in 1815.

The majority of people, however, did not attend any church very regularly and, for many, alcohol provided a more immediate and easier form of release from life's worries and hardships. And condemnation of this was about the only thing that could be guaranteed to unite the different religious groups. Most prominent, of course, was the Temperance Society set up in Preston by the prosperous cheese factor, Radical publisher and reformer, Joseph Livesey. In the town in 1833 he and John King were the first to take the pledge to total abstinence (the latter's speech impediment was said to have given the movement its catchphrase when he declared that his commitment to the cause was 't-total'). As Livesey himself said, 'Preston was soon regarded as the Jerusalem of Teetotalism from which the word went forth in every direction.' One critic saw it rather differently:

Joseph Livesey.

THE ENGLISH JUGGERNAUT.

> The Temperance fanatics collected another mob on Sunday last, and the Sabbath was again desecrated by their insane proceedings. Indeed, the only way we can account for their intemperate conduct . . . is by supposing that they are always drunk.

The evils of drink as seen in the pages of the Temperance newssheet, *The Struggle*.

St Wilfrid's RC Church, Chapel Street,
Preston: only a few yards off Fishergate, but
hidden away behind the shop frontages.

As the nineteenth century progressed, the increase in leisure time and somewhat higher standards of living led to an immense flourishing of social activities. And whereas earlier, most social life like the theatre and learned societies – but not the Guild – had been more or less the preserve of the better-off residents, later there were innumerable popular social activities – the mechanics' reading rooms, brass bands, dramatic societies. Above all there was sport and Preston North End, made famous through the exploits of the 'Invincibles' and of Tom Finney.

The Co-op movement struck deep roots in Preston. As well as the usual chain of shops through the working-class districts, the Preston Industrial Co-operative Society organised many local activities, donated money to charities, helped poor children to get some education, and had, by 1890, opened no fewer than six reading rooms in the town. At the turn of the century and after, much of this, together with all the other communal activities, helped to stimulate the development of an active Labour

Party in Preston. Keir Hardie stood for the seat in 1900 and, despite the Liberal landslide of 1906, John MacPherson won Preston for Labour. To its credit, Preston Corporation took care to safe-guard the town's open spaces, and several parks were laid out, often by workers laid off during the Cotton Famine of the 1860s. Life and work were still hard, but did become easier and more enjoyable.

The entrance to Avenham Park, with Frenchwood Knoll beyond. Preston is well endowed with parks, partly because of job-creation schemes to prevent rioting during the Cotton Famine.

# CHAPTER SEVEN

# Towards a Prouder Preston?

I N ORDER TO MAINTAIN their independence when the English county councils were established in 1888, sixty of the larger towns, including Preston, were made into 'county boroughs'. Already in 1835 the township of Fishwick had been added to the borough; now the whole area from Five Lane Ends to Grimsargh was

Aerial photograph of the Adelphi area, just one of the early industrialised areas on the outskirts of the town centre which has been flattened since the Second World War. English Martyrs Church on Garstang Road can be seen in the top right-hand corner and St George's Road/Aqueduct Street run from left to right across the picture. The Moor Park Methodist Church can (just) be seen on the top edge of the photograph. The mills are Greenbank and Moor Brook, both now demolished. Several mills were built along the course of the largely culverted Moor Brook. Part of this area is now covered with University halls of residence, and some is still open ground.

included. Fulwood remained separate, as an Urban District, until re-organi-
sation in the early 1970s. As usual, Preston was the administrative centre, not
only of the borough, but also of the new county council.

Preston itself had, by this time, become far more urban, with more public
amenities and buildings; no longer did it look like a village that had out-grown
itself. The market square, for example, took on something approaching its
present appearance. The new Town Hall had been built by 1867, a magnificent
gothic-revival structure designed by Sir George Gilbert Scott. In a retro-
Grecian style which must have clashed more than a little, James Hibbert built
the Harris Museum and Library between 1882 and 1893. A local man and
Alderman of the borough, Hibbert also designed the Fishergate Baptist
Church and St James's (now sadly demolished) on Avenham Lane. Gothic
and Grecian were complemented in 1899 by the Italianate masterpiece, Miller
Arcade (one of the first steel-framed buildings in the country), followed by
the new Post Office building and the Municipal Buildings on Birley Street in
1903. These, with their 1933 extension, were destined to become the town
hall after Scott's town hall tragically burned down in 1947, finally to be
demolished in 1962, exactly 100 years after the first stone had been laid.
Crystal House now graces the site. In 1926 the naval commander at the Battle

The 1926 cenotaph with, beyond, the Sessions House and current Town Hall. To
the left is the main Post Office building. It is interesting to compare the current Market Square with the old, pre-industrial one shown in the map on page 9.

TOWN HALL, PRESTON, LANCASHIRE.

Perhaps one day Crystal House (*inset*) will be loved by Prestonians . . . but I doubt it. Most older Prestonians still mourn the loss of their old Town Hall. At least the Obelisk has been reinstated after serving for many years as a pair of gateposts!

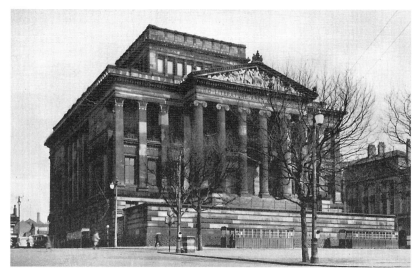

An early postcard view of the Harris Museum (the Miller Arcade had not yet been built). Preston seems to make a habit of designing buildings, like the Guild Hall, with no front door!

Many a Prestonian will remember the archways to the old Town Hall (*left*), a favourite meeting point and bus stop. From 1947, when it burned down, all that remained of this splendid neo-Gothic building were the bottom floors. These were pulled down in 1962 to make way for Crystal House. Notice the Miller Arcade behind, still at this date sporting its cupolas, not sadly gone. A policeman seems to be under-employed on traffic duty as a tram makes its way towards the station with the parish church behind.

of Jutland, Admiral Jellicoe, unveiled the cenotaph on the market square which replaced the earlier South African War memorial of 1904, now in Avenham Park. All this new building did wonders for civic pride, though it did entail the demolition of many older buildings.

The Italianate Miller Arcade, one of the first steel-framed buildings in England, and a beautifully light and airy addition to the town centre.

The cotton industry reached it peak in the decade before the First World War. In Preston it employed nearly 30,000 people. But many developing countries found that cotton manufacture was a relatively simple process, and set up their own industries. This, together with domestic problems and the war itself, broke Lancashire's near monopoly of the trade. After the Great War, production rarely reached pre-war levels, and by the 1950s the industry was in severe decline. Preston was fortunate, however, in having several other industries to fall back on, and was well placed to attract 'replacement industries'. At Red Scar, Courtaulds opened the world's largest rayon plant. In town, English Electric, which had specialised in making tramcars – like the ones which trundled around Preston from 1904 to 1935 – changed to aircraft manufacture during the Second World War and this has become a major employer in the area. Several other engineering firms came to Preston and the surrounding area. Many old mills were converted to new uses. The Albert Edward dock, opened in 1892, was seen as an important asset to the town and, like in medieval times, Preston was a major market, transport and communications centre – the country's first motorway was a by-pass for Preston. The town also developed its service industries, and many office blocks were opened in the town centre.

For the local authorities, the legacy of nineteenth-century expansion and growth lay in huge areas of poor housing, inadequate roads and lack of public amenities like schools and hospitals. Housing, especially after the 1939–45 war, was seen as the most urgent and serious problem. Council estates had been built during the inter-war period, as at Ribbleton where the planners managed to get away from the terraces by building in circles, but almost nothing had been done to tackle the problem of deficient and unfit housing in the older parts of the central area. The effect of leaving the problem for so long was that, during the 1950s and 1960s, it was tackled with too much haste and too little foresight. Close-knit communities, and even quite a lot of decent housing, were swept away along with the slums.

'Towards a Prouder Preston' was the title of a planning document submitted by the Borough Engineer and Surveyor in 1946. Its provisions, fortunately few of which were implemented, were grandiose and would have transformed the entire town centre. It planned to convert or demolish Miller Arcade and many old buildings which, it was claimed, 'to-day have no right to occupy . . . valuable sites'! A huge civic centre near Pole Street, to which a wide 'Processional Way' was to run from Lancaster Road, a university, a hospital, a massive sports and recreational complex by the river and an industrial estate to fill the whole of Fishwick Bottoms were all part of the

Of course Preston needs office space . . . but how could such a carbuncle (*right*) have been allowed to occupy such a prominent site overlooking the river? Right next to the former Park Hotel, one of the grandest on the west-coast line, this modern office block is, ironically, partly occupied by the County Planning Department!

A rather more successful piece of post-war architecture, the Guild Hall was completed just too late to host the 1972 Guild (the Public Hall belatedly being brought back into use instead). Ignore the jokes about it having just landed from outer space, the slightly unhappy relationship with the shopping centre at its heart, and the fact it has no front door, and this building, with its excellent facilities, has earned a place of affection in the hearts of many, perhaps most, Prestonians.

Preston Royal Infirmary on Meadow Street/Deepdale Road, shortly before
beginning its current renovation works.

scheme. One wonders if the council ever gave such an immense plan serious
consideration.

During the twentieth century, Preston has not grown at anything like the
rate it did during the nineteenth. Rather, in fact, more and more people have
moved out from the centre into more open and pleasant areas in Fulwood,
Penwortham and elsewhere. Although this trend has now begun to slacken,
and may even be in reverse, the old centre of Preston now has fewer people
living in it than 500, perhaps 1,000 years ago!

Charles Dickens, in *Hard Times*, said of Coketown

> it is a town of red brick, or of brick that would have been red if the smoke
> and ashes had allowed it; but, as matters stood it was a town of unnatural
> red and black like the painted face of a savage.

In the Preston of the later twentieth century, it is becoming harder and harder
to imagine what Preston was like 100 years ago. Fewer terraced streets are
being pulled down now than during the 1950s and 1960s, and there are still

parts of the town, just away from the central area, that have changed little, but we are a long way from the Preston of John Horrocks, of Joseph Livesey or of Thomas Winckley. And if it is difficult to imagine Preston 100 years ago, how much more difficult it is to think of Preston before the arrival of industry?

# *Further Reading*

Until David Hunt's major new (1992) *History of Preston*, no full town history had been written for half a century, and one still had to rely on Charles Hardwick's capable work of 1857, and on Henry Fishwick's *History of the Parish of Preston* of 1913. The Reference Library in the Harris Museum contains a great mine of local historical material, and one could do much worse than to browse there. The excellent Local History catalogue is the best guide.

The early period is the least well documented, and apart from the general works, it is best to search the pages of the local societies, for example the Historic Society of Lancashire and Cheshire, the Antiquarian Society and the Chetham Society, for more detailed articles. The work of historians like G. H. Tupling, J. D. Marshall, J. J. Bagley and R. Cunliffe Shaw is all useful. For the parish church, Tom C. Smith wrote a good account in 1892, and J. Lingard's book of 1821 is still the fullest guide to the old charters of the town. The *Victoria County History*, of course, contains much valuable material. For the Civil Wars, Ernest Broxap's general work is very good; the Chetham Society in 1844 (vol. ii) printed the *Civil War Tracts* which are very useful. Richard Kuerden's *Brief Description* is available in various editions.

There is too much material for the later period to list here. Again, the shelves of the Harris Reference Library is the best starting point. In particular, there are several university theses on the area which are very useful, and can be found there. Those of K. M. Spencer and Nigel Morgan are especially useful. The Lancashire County Record Office also contains a large amount of material. It has a published several useful guides.

# *Acknowledgements*

The majority of the illustrations in this book are either by the author or from his collection. Special thanks, however, are due to the Harris Museum in Preston, who allowed me access to photograph certain items in their collection, notably the illustrations on pages 3 and 12. The Harris Reference Library kindly gave permission for the photograph on page 49 to be reproduced; Lancashire Record Office kindly gave permission to reproduce the following: the 1715 Fight map, DDX 74/15, and the 1684 manuscript map of Ribbleton, DDX 194/28, are reproduced by kind permission of the County Archivist; the Preston Lock-Out cartoon, DDPr 138/87b, the Cotton Lords of Preston song-sheet, DDPr 138/87a, and the plan of the Market Place, DDPr 141/20, are reproduced by courtesy of the proprietors of the *Lancashire Evening Post*; The sections of Shakeshaft's map, DDHe 122/31, are reproduced by courtesy of The Rt Hon. the Lord Hesketh.

The publishers have made every effort to identify and contact copyright holders, and apologise if any acknowledgement has been omitted.